EVA TOLIMIR

Career Through Contacts

Networking for Women Who Want to Get to the Top

First edition

This book was professionally typeset on Reedsy.
Find out more at reedsy.com

Contents

1

1. Introduction

"No, coffee mornings like that are not for me," said my colleague when I asked her if she wanted to come to the network meeting with me. This left me completely perplexed. The "coffee party" was a meeting of a large network for high-potential women. High-ranking guests were invited and only women who had previously been accepted into the circle of future managers were allowed to attend. It was an opportunity to exchange ideas with women who had made a remarkable career and to learn from each other how women make a career. And that should just be dismissed?

Later, through the research for my dissertation, I learned that networking is a decisive success factor for women's careers. Nevertheless, many people don't like networking. Personally, however, I think it is important and experience, even as a self-employed person, how essential a good network is. This book will look at what networking means and how to build a strategic network. How to build networks in male-dominated environments and how to maintain such a network will also be covered. This book will show you how this can work for you.

First, however, we will explore the question of what networking actually is. In the following, the terms will be used interchangeably and synonymously.

2

2. The basics of networking

Networking is an important success factor for successful careers. However, as you have already experienced, it is not necessarily very popular with women. This is not only a shame, but also a fatal mistake. After all, careers are much easier if you know the right people and can use your contacts properly. But what exactly is networking? And does it have anything to do with coffee mornings?

2.1. What is networking really?

Networking means establishing, maintaining and cultivating the right contacts. However, it goes far beyond small talk and exchanging business cards. It is a strategy to create professional relationships that support a career and are mutually beneficial. Especially for career-oriented women, networking proves to be a powerful tool. I can tell that you are one of these women by the fact that you are holding this book in your hands.

Networking not only enables you to make contacts, but also to take advantage of opportunities that often remain invisible without a network. Networking means building long-term, valuable relationships based on trust, support and common interests. It opens doors and promotes the exchange of knowledge and resources. Together we can overcome challenges better and seize opportunities together. Shared knowledge and recommendations help us make better progress. Networking connects people with similar values and interests who can benefit together through exchange.

The myth of the "natural network"

Many people, especially women, believe that it is enough to let networking happen spontaneously. You simply meet the right people "on your own". This often leads to a passive approach that leaves opportunities untapped. Some female colleagues believe that doing a good job alone is enough for career success. They are often stuck for their entire professional life and do not make any progress. This is the "busy bee" type. In contrast, there are people who consciously select, establish and maintain contacts. Networking therefore requires planning and initiative. It is a conscious, often strategic process that does not necessarily require you to be a "networker type". Nevertheless, the performance must also be right if you want to make a career. Just knowing the right people is not enough.

Successful networking therefore utilizes your own style and strengths in building relationships. The benefits of a strong network are manifold. It offers exclusive information on job offers, industry trends or cooperation opportunities. These opportunities are often worth their weight in gold, as coveted positions are often already filled before they are even advertised. A network can also promote your skills, provide feedback and enable further training through learning from others. In male-dominated industries, a strong network helps to increase visibility and make an appearance where women are otherwise often underrepresented.

A colleague told me how she found out about a vacancy that was coming up through a conversation in the coffee kitchen. Her good relationship with a head of department helped her to apply in good time and then get the job. Networking is often misunderstood as purely selfishly collecting contacts and using them to one's own advantage. But a healthy network is based on reciprocity. You don't just take, you also give. Networking is not a one-sided investment, but an opportunity for valuable relationships that benefit everyone involved. The right mindset in networking is therefore crucial. Overall, networking unfolds its potential if it is used consciously and wisely. It is particularly valuable for ambitious women because it promotes professional development and growth. A strong network can open up career paths, offer support and advance your own career. And as a woman, you are certainly also interested in using these advantages for yourself and not just leaving them to the men.

2.2. Why women need specific strategies

Women often face different challenges than men when it comes to networking. Gender stereotypes, social expectations and different network dynamics influence the way women build and maintain relationships. However, reality shows that networking is an indispensable tool for women to improve their career opportunities and overcome their challenges. In order to pursue this path in a targeted and successful manner, you need specific strategies that do justice to the special circumstances and potential of women.

But what are the actual challenges for women in networking? In the professional environment, women are often confronted with unconscious prejudices and stereotypes. Studies have shown that women are more reserved when it comes to self-promotion and networking, as they often unconsciously conform to social expectations. In addition, women often feel uncomfortable being perceived as "self-centered" when they emphasize their successes or make targeted contacts. After all, this is also part of networking. Presenting and showing yourself as an interesting network partner. Too much restraint in this area can lead to women missing out on important opportunities for career development.

Another challenge is that networks in many industries - especially in male-dominated ones - are often based on informal structures that make it difficult for women to gain access to the key networking circles. Exclusive groups emerge in which men promote and support each other. It is often a hurdle for women to make targeted connections here, as they are not always perceived as equal "players". And I have also experienced the opposite. Women actively withdraw from such activities because they find them "too childish", the slogans too flippant, the tone inappropriate. Sometimes women simply find it too difficult to find the time for such activities. For mothers in particular, but not only, everyday life is usually very busy and full. Going out for an after-work drink with colleagues is not easy. That's why the way women and men network sometimes differs.

Women often build networks that are less hierarchical and more focused on support and exchange than those of men. It is important to me here that we are only talking about tendencies; these aspects should never be generalized. However, these networks are often more resilient and provide a strong backbone for times when support is particularly important. In male-dominated networks, the primary focus is often on getting each other ahead quickly. Female networks tend to only really develop after long-term relationships (you don't want to burden and take advantage of the other person) and focus on common interests and mutual help. However, this does not mean that these networks are less effective. Quite the opposite: these supportive relationships often provide a reliable basis for overcoming challenges at work and creating new opportunities. As already mentioned, it is important to note that male and female networks often have different purposes.

Building targeted female networks brings advantages that go beyond the classic networking goals. Connecting with other women who share similar career goals and challenges creates valuable synergies. These networks can provide mutual support and create a safe environment to discuss topics such as career planning, salary negotiations and work-life balance.

In order to exploit the full potential of networking, women can develop specific strategies to counteract the challenges mentioned:

1. Conscious self-marketing

Women who currently still find this difficult can learn to see self-marketing as a form of positive expression that is not perceived as "self-congratulation". Rather, it is about sharing skills and successes authentically, but also confidently. It can help to focus on the value you offer others. In this way, women can develop a self-confident appearance that inspires and convinces others.

2. Networking with clear goals

Instead of passively waiting for opportunities, women can select networking circles that match their professional goals and proactively build relationships. A strategic network is not only based on sympathy, but on a conscious selection of people who share similar goals, interests or values. By setting clear goals, you can build a network that offers support even in challenging times. This can be part of your own career campaign, so to speak.

3. Find allies and create synergies

Women can look for allies in various networks, including those dominated by men. This means looking for like-minded people who are willing to offer cooperation and support, and overcoming any existing barriers together. By supporting each other and targeting male allies, women can create stronger networks that work effectively even in male-dominated fields.

4. Use female role models

Role models are a powerful tool for overcoming barriers and finding inspiration for your own path. Women who have already successfully built up networks can therefore serve as a source of inspiration. Through the stories and strategies of these women, others learn how challenges can be overcome and career goals successfully achieved. This is not only useful in male business environments, but also in relation to topics that often still mainly affect women. I am thinking, for example, of the topic of career and family. But career and care are also becoming more relevant. I am not saying that this topic is not important for men. However, many studies have shown for years that these aspects still tend to concern women more than men.

Women often need specific strategies in networking in order to take full advantage of the benefits and overcome existing barriers. Through conscious self-marketing, targeted networking and building supportive relationships, many challenges can be overcome. Women can thus create strong networks that not only advance their careers, but also provide an environment in which they can develop personally and professionally. A stable and helpful network is therefore not only a career tool for women, but can also be a source of strength and cohesion.

2.3. How to overcome mental barriers

Building a successful network requires self-confidence and a clear idea of your own strengths and goals. For many women, however, networking is associated with mental barriers that prevent them from realizing the full potential of their contacts. These barriers range from self-doubt and the fear of appearing pushy to the worry of being perceived as a "self-promoter" or even a "dazzler". That's why we're now looking at the most common mental barriers and showing how women can build and develop a healthy self-confidence in order to act authentically and confidently when networking.

Self-doubt and the Impostor Syndrome

Many career-minded women experience the so-called Impostor Syndrome, where they question their own successes and abilities and feel that they don't really "know how to do anything". This doubt can significantly impair the ability to build and actively use networks. Even if there are objective successes, many women tend to play down their achievements and present themselves in a rather reserved manner.

However, it must be clearly stated that this problem does not only affect women. Men are also all too familiar with this phenomenon. A few years ago, I worked as an internal agile coach and enjoyed a high reputation in my organization. Apparently, I was doing a pretty good job. One day, I was sitting in a meeting room with an experienced colleague who had previously been a manager and was now also doing the same job. We were waiting for other colleagues to start the meeting. He also had an excellent reputation and was highly regarded by everyone. In my eyes, he was doing a fantastic job. As we sat there, he looked at me and said: "Tell me, do you know that? I often ask myself what happens when the others find out that I can't do anything and ask me what I'm actually doing? I knew this feeling only too well and yes, I had already asked myself this question. What would happen if the others found out? After we both considered each other to be highly competent, the whole thing ended with us reassuring each other how well we were doing our job and that we knew exactly what we were doing. By the time the other colleagues arrived for the meeting, we could only laugh about our doubts.

What does this mean for you? To overcome this self-doubt, it is helpful to realize that impostor syndrome is widespread and affects even experienced managers. The key to overcoming it is to be aware of your own successes and to communicate them. Also get feedback on your successes. This is because they are also perceived by others. And in most cases, others find our successes much more noteworthy than we do ourselves. Instead of focusing on supposed weaknesses, women should learn to recognize and acknowledge their strengths and use them to present themselves confidently in their network.

The fear of being perceived as "intrusive"

One of the most common fears that holds women back from networking is the worry of being perceived as pushy or "needy". This fear is often deeply rooted and based on the idea that proactive outreach and self-presentation may be seen as inappropriate. Women who perceive networking as uncomfortable or "unfeminine" often withdraw and miss out on valuable opportunities.

A helpful change of perspective is to see networking not as "solicitation" or "self-promotion", but as a mutual exchange. Networking means that both sides benefit, and you can express this confidently. Instead of hiding your own light under a bushel, it is advisable to be open about your own goals and interests. See making contact as an opportunity to offer something to others. This creates a positive exchange in which you can show your ambitions without being seen as pushy. And quite honestly, you have a lot to offer a potential network partner. You just need to be clear about what that is. Then don't hesitate to communicate that.

Self-confidence through authenticity

Authenticity is a key factor for successful networking. This is especially true for women, who often feel under pressure to fulfill the expectations of others. Being authentic means showing yourself as you really are and clearly communicating your own potential and values. Women who are authentic radiate self-confidence and attract people who share similar values and goals.

An authentic appearance can also help to overcome self-doubt and use the network strategically. When women learn to accept themselves and their own style, they gain self-confidence and are less influenced by external expectations. This helps to meet people in the network who not only offer professional support, but also create a valuable connection on a personal level.

Courage to market yourself

One obstacle for many women is their reluctance to market themselves and draw attention to their own successes. While men often seem to find this easier, women often find it uncomfortable or "self-centered".

I still remember well that we had a daily stand-up in my team (note: 15-minute short exchange meeting in the team). At the time, I was an agile coach in a company. The day before, I had held a pilot training session with one of my colleagues. When my manager asked me how it had gone and what the feedback had been like, I said: "I think it went quite well". That was exactly how I felt and how I perceived it. My colleague then said: "What nonsense, it went really well...! That was great! It couldn't have gone any better! Everyone was thrilled." The scales fell from my eyes. Not only was my perception less euphoric, I would never have said it like that. Later, I asked myself why that was actually the case. I then decided to see and evaluate things more positively. This realization was a real game changer for my current self-employment and the knowledge of what my work is worth.

This means that without self-promotion, talents and successes remain invisible - even to potential sponsors and supporters in the network. It is therefore helpful to understand your own self-presentation as part of the networking process. Women should see their successes as valuable contributions. This can inspire others and show them what added value you offer. Incorporate concrete examples and successes into conversations in a targeted manner and thus strengthen your own profile in the network. Self-promotion does not have to be intrusive; it can build a bridge to gain recognition and respect through authentic and clear communication.

Your belief is: "Self-praise stinks?" Replace it with "Self-praise is right!". As you probably don't tend to shout your successes too loudly or too euphorically anyway, what you say about yourself is correct and not exaggerated.

Even if you think you are self-confident, it can sometimes be helpful to remind yourself of things or to activate them. So here are some exercises and techniques for strong self-confidence:

1. Keep a success diary

A success diary is a simple method of documenting your own progress and making yourself aware of your own successes on a regular basis. By recording positive events and successes on a daily or weekly basis, your self-confidence grows and enables you to appear more self-assured in networking situations.

2. Mental visualizations

Use your imagination. Mental visualization is an effective way to use your imagination and picture positive networking situations. Seeing yourself in a successful networking situation supports self-confidence and helps to reduce negative thoughts. As the brain cannot distinguish between imagination and reality, you can already see yourself successfully networking and thus take a big step in the right direction. So feel free to go through the conversations with your desired networking partners in your mind.

3. Start conversations proactively

The ability to proactively start conversations, especially with more senior people, is an important networking skill. By practicing making contact in everyday situations and starting conversations with new people, women gradually reduce their fear of networking situations. You have no problem with this? Wonderful. If you still find it difficult, look for specific opportunities to approach people you wouldn't otherwise talk to.

Mental barriers such as self-doubt and the fear of being seen as pushy prevent many women from taking full advantage of networking. But with self-confidence and authenticity, women can overcome these barriers and succeed in networking situations. Through conscious self-promotion and the targeted application of mental techniques, networking becomes a valuable and enriching resource that contributes to long-term professional success and personal growth. Next, we look at the influence of role models on networking.

2.4. Role models and inspiration

Role models and inspiring personalities play a decisive role in every network. Role models help you to see your own goals more clearly, find ways to achieve them and gain inspiration for your own career. For women in particular, it can be motivating to look to other successful women who have overcome similar challenges. This chapter shows how role models and inspiration can help to strengthen your own career and network.

Role models are people who play an inspiring role through their successes, character or experiences and serve as a guide for others. They show what is possible and help you to follow your own path by providing orientation and courage. A role model in your network is often someone you admire professionally or personally and who has achieved something that you also aspire to. Especially in male-dominated industries, where women are often less represented, role models are an important source of motivation. In my research, interviews with women also showed that the lack of such role models was difficult for many, or that female role models were very helpful.

Finding and observing role models in your own network or industry can help you to reflect on yourself and work on your own career planning. They point out paths that you may not have considered yourself and encourage you to seize new opportunities. Just the realization that what you want is possible and can become reality can be inspiring. Even if the road is sometimes rocky, such stories not only convey professional know-how, but also mental strength, perseverance and the ability to find creative solutions.

You can also gain inspiration by reading biographies, watching interviews or attending events where successful women talk about their careers. Observing how other women deal with challenges and discovering their own strengths and abilities in the process can also help you to recognize your own potential more clearly and use it in a targeted manner.

Mentors as personal role models

A mentor can play a particularly close and supportive role as a personal role model. Mentors offer practical advice and targeted support. A mentor who has established herself in a similar professional environment to where you work can pass on her knowledge and show you how to advance your career and overcome challenges.

Building a relationship with a mentor often requires targeted steps. Start with an open exchange about your career goals and ask specifically for experience and advice. Many experienced women are willing to share their knowledge and experience if they recognize that you show genuine interest and commitment. Such a relationship is therefore also valuable for you in the long term and can be a source of support.

To be fair, it must be said at this point that research shows that male mentors actively support the careers of their mentees significantly more often by opening up their own network to their mentees. They recommend their mentees for vacancies more often and are more helpful for career progress overall. Female mentors are more restrictive with this resource. This is particularly unfortunate, as it would be desirable for women to explicitly support other women. Unfortunately, it has to be said that this is not always the case.

Use positive characteristics of role models yourself

Having a role model means recognizing the positive qualities of this person that you would also like to develop for yourself. For example, if you admire a colleague who is always diplomatic and solution-oriented, you can make a conscious effort to develop the same attitude in difficult situations. By specifically observing and analyzing which qualities you find inspiring in your role models, you can work specifically on promoting similar qualities in yourself.

A useful exercise can be to write down the characteristics of your role models and consider how you can integrate them step by step into your own behavior. This helps you to develop an individual version of the best qualities and to orientate yourself towards your personal style. Sometimes it is also helpful to focus and practice one trait per week, for example. Be gracious with yourself if it doesn't work out the way you want it to. After all, Rome wasn't built in a day.

As your career progresses, you too will develop and can become an inspiration to others. By taking on the role of a role model for others, whether through mentoring, sharing your experiences or creating a supportive atmosphere, you will help to establish a culture of encouragement and inspiration in your network. An inspiring attitude and a willingness to support others will not only strengthen your own network, but also enhance your reputation as a valued and trustworthy person.

But remember: when you share your own experiences and successes, you remain authentic and respectful. Every career path is unique, and it is precisely this diversity that makes inspiration valuable. So also talk about setbacks and challenges.

This can help your mentees to paint a realistic picture of an achievable career path and give them courage.

Overall, it can be said that role models and inspiring people in the network provide orientation, support and motivation. By observing and learning from successful women and mentors, you can recognize your own goals more clearly and work specifically on developing your strengths. At the same time, it is valuable to adopt an inspiring attitude yourself and pass on your experiences to serve as a role model for others. In this way, you contribute to a supportive network that enables mutual promotion and growth.

3

3. Strategically building your personal network

3.1. How to analyze your own network

A strong network starts with a clear understanding of existing contacts and their potential. The first step is to systematically analyze your network to identify which relationships are already in place and which additional contacts could be important for achieving professional goals. By analyzing their networks, women can target gaps and strategically expand their contacts to create a network that provides both professional and personal support.

So the first step is to collect and evaluate your existing contacts. Most people have a more extensive network than they realize. Friends, former colleagues, family members, former superiors or study contacts - all of these people are potentially part of a valuable network that can help with professional development.

At the beginning of the analysis, it is helpful to create an overview of existing contacts and also think about less obvious relationships.

An effective approach to this is to create a contact list or organizational chart in which all contacts and their respective relationship to your own career development are recorded. This helps to systematically record the network and possibly rediscover valuable connections that have faded into the background over time. At the same time, this list can be used to determine where there are gaps and where potential contacts are missing that would be helpful in career development.

Then evaluate the quality of the contacts. Which ones bring you professional added value? Who can you add value to? Your comprehensive contact list is the first step, but not every relationship is equally helpful to your professional goals. Networks should consist of different types of relationships that cover specific needs: Mentors who can provide advice and support; colleagues with whom you can share knowledge and experience; or industry experts who can provide valuable insight and information.

In order to assess the quality of the network, existing contacts can be categorized in terms of their added value:

1. mentors and sponsors: contacts who have extensive experience and are willing to share their knowledge, as well as people who have the potential to open doors.

2. colleagues and like-minded people: Contacts who are at the same professional level or share similar experiences and

with whom you can exchange ideas and support each other.

3. sources of inspiration and innovators: contacts that provide creative impetus and enable access to new trends or ideas.

This categorization quickly makes it clear which contacts are particularly valuable for professional ambitions and which connections may be less relevant. In this way, it is possible to specifically determine which relationships should be cultivated and intensified and which contacts may not offer any long-term added value.

Now look at what gaps there may be in your existing network. A balanced network should have contacts from different areas in order to be able to offer support in different subject areas. Networks often consist mainly of contacts who have similar professional backgrounds and perspectives. This can lead to important insights and new opportunities being lost because the network is too homogeneous.

This is therefore an opportunity to consciously diversify your network. Are there industries or positions with which you have few contacts? Do you lack role models or experienced mentors in your field? By specifically looking for new contacts in these areas, you will broaden your perspectives and gain access to knowledge and resources that were previously untapped.

After analyzing your existing network and identifying gaps, you can create a network plan to pursue your goals in a targeted manner. Such a plan should clearly define which contacts you want to build up and how you want to do this. For example, you could set out to gain three experienced industry contacts in the next six months or get involved in networks and groups that give you access to inspiring personalities.

A network plan helps you to approach the networking process in a structured and targeted manner. It enables you to build targeted relationships and keep an eye on which contacts can really help you. This will not only make your network more extensive, but also more targeted and valuable for your career development. This plan can be a visual representation, e.g. in the form of a mind map, or a simple Excel spreadsheet. Use the format that helps you the most. Think about what added value you can bring to networking at this stage.

In conclusion, analyzing your existing network is an important step in strategically supporting your professional goals. By systematically recording and evaluating existing contacts, you can recognize where valuable relationships exist and which gaps should be filled. Drawing up a network plan helps you to expand your network in a targeted and sustainable way in order to build a strong and supportive network for your career goals in the long term.

3.2. Networking strategies

A strong network is characterized by diversity. Successful networking means making targeted contacts in different areas, each of which can contribute to your career in different ways. This chapter shows you how you can build valuable relationships through targeted strategies - from mentoring and collegial networks to external contacts that open up new perspectives and opportunities for you.

Mentoring: finding mentors and building relationships

How do you find a mentor? To find a mentor, it is important to first clarify what kind of support you need. Do you want the mentor to help you with strategic decisions? Or are you looking for someone to help you develop specific skills? If you have clear goals in mind, it will be easier to find a suitable person. Potential mentors could be former superiors, experienced colleagues or managers in your industry, for example.

If you don't know who might be a suitable mentor, talk to your manager. Many companies also offer mentoring programs. Find out what opportunities are available in your company and take advantage of them. Or you can choose a specific person and approach them.

Building such a relationship often starts with informal contact. When approaching someone you would like to mentor, it is helpful to show an interest in their career and experience. Ask specifically for an exchange or an informal conversation to lay the foundation for a long-term, supportive relationship.

Collegial networks: promoting collaboration and achieving common goals

A collegial network consists of contacts at a similar professional level with whom you can exchange information, experiences and challenges. Collegial networks provide an excellent opportunity to support each other and grow together. For women in particular, it can be helpful to create networks with colleagues or peers to discuss career-specific topics, such as salary negotiation or balancing career and family.

To build a collegial network, you can, for example, initiate internal or external groups or join existing networks in which like-minded people with similar interests are represented. A regular exchange, for example through monthly meetings or an online group, strengthens cohesion and enables everyone involved to learn from and motivate each other.

An important strategy in the collegial network is the culture of sharing and giving. Those who are willing to share helpful tips or experiences will often receive support in return. A collegial network should therefore be based on trust and openness in order to function in the long term and offer added value to everyone involved. Plan specific (working) time for this. For most men, networking is a natural part of working hours, whereas women often say: I don't have time for this, I still have work to do. Consider networking as part of your work.

External contacts: Sector-specific and cross-industry networks

While mentors and colleagues can come from your own company or industry, it is equally valuable to build up an external network that extends beyond your own working environment. External contacts provide insights into other industries and often offer inspiring perspectives. They open up access to new ideas and innovations and broaden your own horizons, which is particularly valuable in times of rapid change on the job market.

Industry-specific networks, such as professional associations or specialist events, offer a good opportunity to make targeted contacts within your own field of work. These contacts can support you with specific professional issues and help you to recognize trends and developments at an early stage. They also increase your visibility within the industry and increase the likelihood of being considered for new career opportunities.

In addition, overarching networks that transcend sectors and specialist areas can be particularly enriching. Networks from different industries often offer inspiration and solutions that you would not find within your own industry. This allows you to think outside the box, so to speak. Innovations often arise in precisely this way. These types of contacts can be made, for example, at interdisciplinary conferences or in networks that connect different professional fields, such as career events, innovation forums or alumni meetings.

Networking via social media and LinkedIn

In a digital world, networking via social media is almost indispensable. LinkedIn and other platforms offer excellent opportunities to build up targeted contacts in various fields and maintain them in the long term. Social media allows you to gain visibility, share your own content and make your professional profile appealing to potential contacts.

To make networking via social media successful, it is important to be authentic and active. Share relevant content, comment on your contacts' posts and show interest in their work. On LinkedIn in particular, you can search specifically for people who work in certain industries or companies and contact them with a friendly and professional message. Remember that a first contact works best if you are genuinely interested and want to build a relationship, rather than just collecting another profile. Ask yourself, who is this person? What interesting things does he or she do? How can I benefit this person?

Regularly interacting and sharing content on social platforms not only strengthens existing connections, but also continuously expands your network and allows you to gain new contacts in different areas. It also allows others to find out more about what you are involved in, what is important to them and much more. This also makes you more tangible as a person.

A diverse network of mentors, colleagues and external contacts therefore forms a solid foundation for successful career development. By building targeted relationships in different areas, you create a network that supports you in a variety of challenges and opportunities. Strategically building such networks - from mentoring and collegial relationships to industry-specific and cross-industry contacts - will help you not only achieve your professional goals, but also find inspiration and support along the way. But how do you actually get in touch?

3.3. Effective contact and the magical first impression

First impressions and the way you approach a contact can make or break the success of your networking efforts. An authentic and strategic approach not only leaves a positive first impression, but also lays the foundation for a valuable relationship. In this chapter, you will learn how to initiate contacts effectively and present yourself in a professional and personable manner.

Strategies for the first contact

Making contact often requires some effort. Nevertheless, it is an important step in networking, because a targeted first contact can be invaluable in the long term. Effective outreach starts with a clear goal: ask yourself why you want to make this contact and what you hope to gain from the relationship. The clearer your intention, the easier it is to find the right strategy and open an authentic conversation.

When making initial contact, it can be helpful to address common interests, points of contact or specific professional topics that you both find relevant. Instead of expressing a general interest, you can focus on topics that will enhance the contact and make it interesting from the outset. This will show that you have researched the person and their background and are genuinely interested in an exchange.

What is the best way to do this?
Use informal occasions. Events, conferences or webinars

28

often offer an informal atmosphere to get into conversation. Use breaks or networking sessions to make contacts.

Make sure you also use virtual networks. LinkedIn and other social platforms are particularly suitable for making initial contact. Here you can address the person with a short message and point out similarities. Common contacts or shared areas of work are particularly suitable here.

Listen actively and ask questions. A good conversation thrives on exchange. By asking questions and showing interest, you give the other person space and make it clear that you are genuinely interested in their opinion and experiences. Feel free to take notes on the person after conversations. It's not unusual to only meet someone again after a while. If you're like me, you're genuinely interested in the person but can't remember whether the children are still small or about to finish school. You may also have forgotten the person's last vacation destination. Especially if you often meet new people, you can easily get things mixed up here. Show your appreciation and take two minutes to write down such details so that you can refer back to them the next time you meet.

It is also important for the other person to quickly get a picture of who you are. A clear, authentic elevator pitch helps you to introduce yourself confidently and succinctly at the first meeting. An elevator pitch is a short, meaningful summary of who you are, what you do and what you are currently interested in. The aim is to give a brief and convincing overview of yourself that will be remembered and at the same time lay the foundation for a more in-depth conversation.

A good elevator pitch should summarize your professional identity in 30 to 60 seconds and point out your key strengths or goals. Make sure you remain authentic and don't go over the top. Choose one or two key topics that are important to you and concentrate on these instead of confusing your counterpart with a flood of information. This will keep you clear and focused and leave a professional and likeable impression. You can prepare this elevator pitch in a quiet hour so that you can refer back to it at any time. And this is how you structure a successful elevator pitch:

1. introduction: A simple introduction that draws attention to you (e.g. "Hi, I'm Anna and I've been working in marketing strategy for five years.").

2. your professional role and core competencies: Emphasize what you are good at and what sets you apart (e.g., "I am a team leader and specialize in developing brand strategies that help companies stand out in the marketplace.").

3. your current goal or interest: Clarify what you are currently aiming for or looking for (e.g. "At the moment I am particularly interested in sustainable marketing approaches and am looking forward to learning more about them.").

4. conclude with a reference to the other person: End the pitch with an open question or a connecting point to continue the conversation (e.g. "I've heard that you also work in marketing - what do you think is a key trend in the industry?").

In this way, you can briefly and concisely inform your conversation partners about yourself and also have a topic to continue the conversation with.

Of course, there are many different ways to design an elevator pitch. Formulate your own pitch and check whether you feel comfortable with it.

In addition to the content, the way in which you present yourself also plays a decisive role. It has long been known that first impressions are formed in the first few seconds and are strongly influenced by non-verbal signals. Your appearance, your body language and your voice make a significant contribution to how you are perceived.

A friendly smile, an open posture and a firm handshake (or, in virtual meetings, a clear and upright posture and a smile in front of the camera) show self-confidence and openness. Avoid crossing your arms or turning away too much from the person you are talking to - this could be perceived as closed or insecure. An open gaze and eye contact signal interest and commitment. So be sure to switch on the camera during virtual meetings.

Another factor is your voice: a calm, clear voice makes a confident impression and conveys security. If you are nervous, it can help to speak slowly and breathe consciously to appear calm and collected. This way you can ensure that your first impression is positive and inviting. Are you still unsure about body language? Are you still unsure about how you come across? That's not a bad thing. Get a book about it or book a course and get ideas and feedback.

Authenticity is an important aspect of first contact. People can sense whether someone is being authentic or trying to play a role. The contact will be more valuable if you show yourself as you are and openly address your own strengths and interests.

Be honest about what you are looking for and what you can offer instead of pretending. Authenticity creates trust and makes you appear as a credible and reliable person. Sometimes it can also be appropriate to set yourself apart and clearly show what you may not be good at. This can sometimes save both parties a lot of time.

An authentic appearance also means recognizing and accepting boundaries. If a conversation stalls or you have the feeling that there is no mutual interest, there is no need to worry. Not every contact will necessarily lead to a valuable relationship, and it's okay if not every contact turns out to be suitable.

You will surely have recognized this: The first contact lays the foundation for a valuable relationship and can be decisive for the further course of your networking efforts. With a clear and targeted approach, an authentic elevator pitch and a confident first impression, you create the basis for trusting relationships. An attentive appearance, friendly body language and authentic communication are the keys to making a positive and lasting impression.

3.4. Expand your network in a targeted manner

You already know that an existing network is a valuable career asset, but a really strong network is constantly changing and evolving. A targeted expansion of your network opens up new opportunities, promotes exchange and brings new perspectives. In this chapter, you will learn how to expand your network in a targeted manner in order to gain valuable new contacts and build long-term relationships - whether through events, digital platforms or targeted social media strategies.

Professional events and conferences are excellent opportunities to make new contacts. These opportunities not only provide access to specialist knowledge, but also allow you to meet people with similar interests and goals. It is helpful to develop a strategy in advance to get the most out of the event.

Even before a conference or event, it makes sense to familiarize yourself with the list of participants and the programme, if these are available. Think about who you would like to talk to and prepare a brief introduction to your own interests or professional profile. Also think about your elevator pitch here. A targeted conversation starter can be, for example, a specific interest in a speaker's presentation or a question about a participant's area of expertise. Such approaches make the first conversation easier and help you get straight into the topic.

During the event, it can be useful to exchange business cards or contact details, but also to establish a direct connection via LinkedIn. After the event, you should contact the new contacts briefly and, for example, refer to common topics of conversation or interesting points from the event. A short message helps to strengthen the connection and secure the exchange in the long term. Here too, follow the tip from above to take notes on the conversations. This way, you will have everything to hand for later meetings. But you can also expand your network virtually.

Social media - especially LinkedIn - is indispensable today for continuously expanding your network. LinkedIn allows you to search specifically for people who are active in relevant industries, companies or positions and with whom you would like to make contact. A well-maintained profile and regular activities on the platform help to increase your visibility and underline your professionalism.

To attract new contacts via LinkedIn, you can, for example, share specialist articles, post comments under relevant articles and actively participate in discussions. By sharing content and demonstrating your expertise, you position yourself as an expert in your field and attract potential contacts who are interested in similar topics.

If you want to approach a person specifically, send a personal message explaining why you are interested in an exchange. A simple, personal reference - such as a mention of a common professional topic or a comment that the person has recently posted - shows that you are genuinely interested in the contact.

If you are well networked, you will also have contacts in various industries and specialist areas. Even if it makes sense to maintain a strong network in your own industry, it can be particularly enriching to think outside the box and network with people from other areas.

At innovation or management conferences, for example, you can get to know people who work in completely different areas but share similar professional values or interests. Participation in cross-industry events or involvement in networks that unite different industries gives you access to contacts that can provide new impetus. These contacts often bring valuable ideas and insights that are rarely found in an industry-specific network.

Another good way to expand your network is through networking groups or professional associations, as they are designed to bring people with common interests together and encourage the building of valuable relationships. Professional associations often offer regular meetings, lectures and events where contacts can not only be made but also intensified.

In addition, there are many specialized groups aimed at specific professional groups or areas of interest, e.g. groups for women in management, women starting out in their careers, female founders or specific specialist areas such as marketing, finance or IT. The exchange in such groups creates a close network of like-minded people who encourage and support each other.

Of course, networking does not end with the first contact. In order to really benefit from new contacts and expand the network, it is crucial to maintain these relationships in the long term. This means staying in regular contact and showing an interest in the other person's developments.

For example, set yourself the goal of getting in touch with each key contact a few times a year. Whether it's a quick email, a message on LinkedIn or a phone call, small tokens of appreciation like this help to keep the contact alive. If you have the opportunity to attend a meeting in person or virtually, take the opportunity to take the conversation further. Show an interest in your contacts' developments and also offer support or recommendations yourself if you can.

Such regular interactions turn a simple contact into a valuable relationship that will endure into the future. Long-term networks can be an invaluable source of inspiration and support that remains useful for many years to come.

For you, this means that the targeted expansion of your network requires a strategic approach and a willingness to engage with new people. Whether through events, social networks or networking groups - expanding your network not only opens up new professional opportunities, but also provides valuable impetus and perspectives. The long-term cultivation of these new relationships strengthens the network in the long term and makes it an important resource for your career.

4

4. Networking in male-dominated environments

4.1. The special features of male-dominated networks

etworking in male-dominated industries poses specific challenges for women. In such environments, traditional network structures and informal "rules of the game" have often developed, which can make it difficult for women to gain access to important contacts and decision-making processes. This chapter sheds light on the special features that characterize male-dominated networks and shows strategies on how women can navigate these structures effectively and integrate successfully.

Network culture and rules in male-dominated industries

Male-dominated industries, such as finance, technology or

engineering, often have network structures based on informal and often traditional rules. These networks are regularly based on "old boys' clubs" - informal circles and meetings where important decisions and agreements are made, to which women have little or no access. Such networks have developed over years and tend to rely heavily on personal loyalties and long-standing relationships, making it difficult for outsiders and women in particular to get involved.

A first step in understanding these networks and finding your way around them is to observe and understand the dynamics: How and where are decisions made? What informal meetings or events take place regularly that could give you access to key networks? Knowing this can help you to seize opportunities and position yourself accordingly.

The invisible rules of the game: What men often do differently

We've seen it before: Men and women often differ in their networking behavior. While women tend to build networks based on common interests and a strong exchange of ideas, male-dominated networks are often characterized by targeted, pragmatic connections. In male-dominated networks, contacts are often actively used to gain career advancement opportunities or access to exclusive information. Men are also less likely to show inhibitions about openly communicating their own interests and actively requesting support.

It can be helpful for women to become aware of some of these pragmatic approaches and, if necessary, integrate them into their own networking behavior. This does not mean adapting completely, but rather adopting specific elements that could be useful in a male-dominated environment. For example, having the courage to formulate clear professional goals and communicate these within the network is an aspect that is taken for granted in male-dominated networks and can also help women to present their ambitions and skills in a targeted manner.

So the question arises as to how you can still become part of these networks. As women are still in the minority or not represented at all in many male-dominated industries, it can be useful to apply a strategy of subtle integration. This means consciously fitting into existing structures without losing your own identity and authenticity. Subtle integration can be achieved through targeted participation in informal meetings, networking events or even by sharing common interests - for example through sports, lunch together or interests such as business topics and industry discussions, which often characterize informal networks in male industries.

You can achieve this by focusing specifically on certain members of a network who can act as a "bridge". These people are often open to new contacts and can establish a connection to other network members. By building trust and interest in these relationships, you create a basis for integrating yourself into the network bit by bit. It is helpful to find a balance between adapting and being authentic in order to gain the acceptance of the network and maintain your own style. Be patient here, this relationship building can take a while.

In male-dominated networks, it is also particularly important to have a clear professional positioning and to communicate this confidently. Unfortunately, women in such networks are often only perceived in supporting roles or supporting positions. To break through this perception, it is crucial to emphasize your own skills and goals openly and purposefully.

It can help to regularly make your own successes visible and actively participate in discussions. Demonstrating your expertise in presentations or meetings and being present for critical decisions increases your visibility and influence within the network. Being an expert in a certain field can also help you to be recognized as a valuable resource within the network. If you are not yet used to presenting yourself as a competent contact person, don't be afraid to change this. Positioning yourself in this way can consolidate your status in the network in the long term and improve your opportunities for professional development.

Define a tactic for yourself to deal with inappropriate communication that you are not comfortable with. In a male-dominated environment, it is to be expected that you will not always like what is discussed and how it is discussed.

In a workshop in which I was a facilitator, I once had a wonderful experience with this type of communication. The participants were all men, doctors, each of whom headed a different department in a large clinic. They were therefore all high-ranking managers, who could certainly be described as alpha males. We had a tight schedule and at a set time we had to switch back to the plenary session for the next slot. One participant was visibly unhappy about being regularly limited in his speaking time by a woman. He was probably just not used to it. Within a very short time, he made more and more comments that clearly showed how he felt about it. At some point, he said succinctly to the group: well, she's pretty stubborn. I stayed calm, looked at him and just said: "Of course. You know how women are.". The room immediately erupted in laughter. What I didn't know was that this colleague was the head of gynecology. One of the other participants then said that he should finally admit defeat and let me do my job. Even the grumpy participant had to laugh about it and we were able to continue working purposefully. What I want to tell you is this: stay calm and appreciative, but don't give in either.

In male-dominated industries, your challenge is often to gain access to existing network structures and position yourself effectively within them. Through observation and subtle integration, women can make targeted use of these structures without losing their authenticity. Clear positioning and the courage to communicate professional goals and successes make a significant contribution to increasing your own visibility and recognition. Supporters and allies in the network are a valuable resource for successfully navigating male-dominated networks in the long term and establishing yourself as a competent and self-confident partner.

4.2. Finding strategic alliances and supporters

For women who want to advance their career, it can be particularly helpful to gain strategic alliances and supporters. They support you in your professional development and increase your visibility. An alliance not only means having valuable connections, but also pursuing common goals, strengthening each other and sticking together in challenging situations. The following is about how you can specifically find alliances and supporters and build and maintain these relationships.

In our case, strategic alliances are relationships that help you to achieve your career goals in a targeted manner and gain influence in the industry or company. Unlike traditional contacts, alliances are characterized by a higher level of commitment and mutual support. In an alliance, both parties commit to actively promoting each other, be it through knowledge, recommendations or introductions to relevant networks.

Alliances are particularly valuable when they are built with people who have valuable resources or networks. In male-dominated industries, such connections can be crucial in gaining access to exclusive information and career opportunities that would otherwise be difficult to access. A strategic alliance allows you to bring your own skills and strengths to the network while benefiting from the resources and knowledge of your counterpart.

In such alliances, it makes sense to look for both female and male supporters. Male allies can act as allies and help to expand spheres of influence, gain access to key networks and overcome barriers. Male supporters who understand the importance of diversity and equality can give women an important voice in male-dominated industries. If you manage to recruit such a male supporter, you will be surprised at what he will do to help you.

A valuable approach to gaining such male allies is, as already mentioned, to talk clearly and openly about your own goals and challenges. By starting the conversation about shared interests and values, you can create a basis on which to develop a working relationship. Such an exchange promotes mutual understanding and shows that working together can be beneficial for both sides. Men also appreciate it when women clearly formulate their goals.

At the same time, networking and building alliances with other women in the industry is invaluable. Female supporters understand the particular challenges and experiences women face in male-dominated networks and can offer valuable advice, experience and support. Such relationships foster mutual empowerment and create a network in which women can empower and support each other.

An alliance is particularly strong when it is based on common goals. These can be professional interests, personal values or specific projects where the skills of both sides complement each other perfectly. By building potential alliances with people who have similar values or goals, collaboration not only becomes more natural, but also more sustainable.

Start by approaching potential partners and talking about how a collaboration can help both sides. This could be joint projects, training courses or the contribution of specific skills, for example. Identifying common goals makes it easier to shape the collaboration in a targeted manner and thus contribute to mutual added value. People who pursue similar interests are often more willing to make a long-term commitment and actively promote the relationship.

Trust is the foundation of every successful alliance. People are more likely to enter into relationships if they have the feeling that their counterpart is reliable and is looking for a genuine connection. Building trust requires time, honesty and a willingness to give support without expecting anything in return.

It is particularly useful to proactively contribute your own knowledge and resources. By offering support to potential allies, e.g. by sharing information, recommendations or specific expertise, you can strengthen trust and show that you take the relationship seriously. Small gestures of support - such as honest feedback, a helpful contact or advice - signal to your counterpart that you are not only interested in personal gain, but also in long-term cooperation. Maintaining an alliance is therefore just as important as building one in the first place. Keep in regular contact and show an interest in your counterpart's developments. An occasional meeting or a joint project can also help to maintain and strengthen the relationship.

Mentoring has already been mentioned in the previous chapters. It is also an important aspect of building strategic alliances. Sponsors or mentors can be instrumental in helping women grow and achieve their goals in male-dominated industries. A sponsor is someone who not only shares knowledge, but also actively contributes to the advancement of your career -

be it through recommendations, visibility in the company or involvement in specific projects.

Overall, strategic alliances and supporters play a central role in successful networking, especially in male-dominated industries. Women can improve their chances of gaining access to key networks and decisions through targeted alliances and finding supporters. By attracting both male and female supporters and building these relationships based on trust and common goals, you create a stable network that will accompany and support you in the long term. Building and maintaining such relationships takes time and commitment, but provides a valuable long-term resource for your career development.

4.3. Gaining visibility and recognition

In male-dominated industries and networks, it is often a challenge to become visible as a woman and to receive the recognition that does justice to one's own skills and achievements. As networks in such environments are often informal and based on traditional structures, it is particularly important to actively strive for your own visibility and to showcase your expertise in a targeted manner. That is why we are now looking at how you can increase your professional presence and gain recognition for your work.

An important strategy for standing out in male-dominated networks is an authentic and self-confident appearance. Perhaps you also tend to play down your successes or present your achievements less prominently. We have already talked about this in this book. However, in order to become truly visible in an industry or network, it is necessary to speak confidently about your achievements and skills. Really take this to heart.

A clear first step is to regularly communicate your own skills and goals, whether in meetings, through presentations or in discussions with colleagues and superiors. If you are working on projects that are going particularly well or if you achieve important results, you should also communicate this clearly and directly. Sometimes it can be useful not to present your successes solely as a personal achievement, but always in the context of team performance or the company's goal, to show authenticity and a team-oriented attitude. If you are unsure about what you can communicate, think back to the success diary. Never present a team achievement as your own, but don't hide your light under a bushel either.

Increase your chances of being perceived as a competent contact person by communicating special projects or topics that you are working on. Such "lighthouse projects" or special-izations serve as a figurehead and make it easier for others to recognize your role and your value in the network.

Think about which projects or topics you are particularly interested in and in which you have specialist knowledge. Create opportunities to showcase this expertise, for example by volunteering for a project where you can demonstrate your skills. Offering a lecture, workshop or training course can also help others to notice and recognize your knowledge in a particular area.

Also take advantage of networking events and informal meetings, as many contacts and decisions are made in such contexts. Attending these events is often a crucial factor in being visible and taking advantage of opportunities that arise outside the formal work context. These are opportunities to make your presence felt and to specifically address your professional interests and projects in conversations with other participants. In addition, we usually remember people we have met in person better than people from virtual networks.

If you find it difficult to open conversations, you can use simple icebreakers, for example by asking questions about current projects or topics that are relevant to the event. By showing interest, you create a basis for stimulating conversations in which you can also subtly incorporate your own perspectives and successes.

We have already talked about social media in a previous chapter. These platforms are also important for visibility and self-marketing. LinkedIn, for example, allows you to share your achievements and knowledge with a wider network and clearly communicate your professional interests. By sharing posts, commenting on relevant topics and publishing your own articles, you can highlight your expertise and raise your profile.

A strategic digital presence can help you to be noticed by important people in your network, even if you have little direct contact on a day-to-day basis. Think about which topics are relevant to your industry and your role and share content that positions you as a competent contact person. It is helpful to remain authentic and to design your posts in such a way that they reflect your personality.

You can also gain visibility and recognition by actively participating in meetings and discussions. In male-dominated networks or teams, it can be challenging to make yourself heard, especially when male colleagues are more dominant. It can be helpful to prepare specifically for meetings, plan your own contributions in advance and address specific points that emphasize your expertise. Stay persistent and don't let yourself be boxed out!

Another way to ensure visibility in meetings is to ask specific questions or respond to relevant points made by other participants. This type of active participation not only shows that you are well prepared, but also that you are engaging with the contributions of others. This can help you to be perceived as a valuable voice in the room and gain recognition for your constructive participation.

What if the meetings are the scene of competition and power games? This can certainly make life difficult for you. In such situations, it is important to keep calm and focus on your strengths without getting involved in competitive battles. Instead, use professional courtesy and focus on factual arguments and your own expertise.

If you are met with subtle devaluations or ignorant comments, it is advisable to remain calm and objective. Try to show your competence calmly and do not engage in defensive behavior. If you continuously and confidently present your strengths, those around you will recognize your competence and steadfastness in the long term. So keep at it and don't give up.

Gaining visibility and recognition in male-dominated networks requires strategic and proactive action. By clearly communicating your successes, focusing on specific topics and projects and having a professional digital presence, you can position yourself successfully. Active participation in meetings, networking events and a self-confident way of presenting yourself will help you to consolidate your role in the network and be recognized as a competent contact in the long term.

4.4. Confident appearance and networking with style

A self-confident appearance and an authentic style are crucial in order to be successful in networks - especially in male-dominated industries. Such an appearance is based on a clear self-awareness, the ability to confidently show your own strengths and the willingness to maintain your own individual style. This chapter will give you further ideas on how to develop self-confidence while remaining authentic so that you are perceived as a competent and trustworthy personality in your network.

Self-confidence, as we already know, starts with a clear knowledge of your skills and strengths. Especially in networks where women are often still in the minority, it is important to have solid confidence in your own abilities. Being aware of your own skills gives you the security to represent your ideas and opinions confidently and not be easily unsettled by external circumstances. You can also use the success journal to further boost your self-confidence. It will also help you to be more aware of your successes and to be able to mention them where necessary.

Your body language is an essential part of a confident appearance and influences how others perceive you. An upright posture, an open gaze and calm gestures signal self-confidence and aplomb. Especially in challenging networking situations or conversations with dominant personalities, you can consciously use your body language to show presence and strength.

Make sure you maintain eye contact during conversations and keep your posture open, for example by not crossing your arms and turning towards the other person. Your voice also sends out signals. So speak calmly and clearly, this will make you appear confident. As already mentioned, speaking slowly and breathing consciously can help. This allows you to remain calm and formulate your statements clearly and confidently. These non-verbal signals support your appearance and add weight to your words.

There is often pressure for women to adapt in male-dominated networks and change their own style in favor of the established "rules of the game". However, you will be most successful in the long term if you remain authentic and maintain your own style. Authenticity creates trust and credibility - two important factors for building long-term relationships and being respected in the network. Here I would like to invite you once again to consider what kind of communication you personally feel comfortable with and also where your individual boundaries lie. Even if you may not like to hear this: Men communicate with each other differently. If you want to establish yourself in such a context, you may also have to venture out of your comfort zone. You have to decide for yourself whether and to what extent this makes sense and is acceptable for you personally.

So instead of pretending or showing characteristics that don't match your personality, it makes sense to focus on your own strengths. If you are more reserved, you can use this as a strength by listening well to others and making carefully worded contributions. If, on the other hand, you are extroverted, you can show a natural presence by being open and communicative. You may have heard the saying: one man, one word, one woman, one dictionary. Frankly, my experience clearly shows that men also love to talk. I would therefore like to emphasize once again that listening well can be a valuable quality. On the one hand, it helps to build a relationship, and on the other, you may gain valuable insights. But stay true to yourself.

Networking with style means treating others with respect and appreciation. Appreciative communication creates a positive atmosphere and helps you to be remembered. This includes not only polite manners, but also active listening and genuine interest in the perspectives of others. When you communicate openly and respectfully, you signal that you take the relationship seriously and see the network as a mutual resource.

Good networking style also means behaving fairly and collegially. Even when competitive situations arise, you should always remain professional and fair and refrain from more or less subtle power games. If you are always constructive and positive in decisions and discussions, this will strengthen your position in the network in the long term and establish you as a respected partner.

Mastering difficult situations with confidence

In male-dominated networks, you may be confronted with challenging situations or dominant personalities. Remain calm in such moments and maintain your composure. One way to do this is to focus on the actual goal of the conversation and not let yourself be rattled by possible provocations or power games.

If you find yourself in a situation where your competence is questioned or you feel uncomfortable, clear, fact-based answers or targeted questions can help. By defending your position objectively and remaining calm, you show that you will not be upset. This kind of behavior strengthens your credibility in the long term and signals to your conversation partners that you are a competent and trustworthy person.

Self-confidence in self-marketing

A self-confident appearance also includes the ability to market yourself confidently. Especially in male-dominated environments, it is important to make your own successes and skills visible in a targeted manner. This does not mean "selling" yourself, but rather presenting and emphasizing your skills appropriately. Self-marketing can be done discreetly and subtly, for example by specifically mentioning projects or successes that fit in with current topics.

A useful approach is to target opportunities for self-promotion - be it in meetings, at networking events or when talking to managers. If you recognize an opportunity where your skills are relevant, you can address this and confidently make your contributions. In this way, you signal that you are taking on an active role and are prepared to take on responsibility.

A confident appearance and authentic networking are therefore essential to be successful in male-dominated networks. Strong self-confidence, conscious body language and an appreciative tone of voice help you to stand out positively in the network. Through authenticity and respectful interaction, you create trust and credibility in the long term, which gives you recognition and influence in the network. The strategic use of your strengths and confident self-marketing round off a stylish and successful appearance and lay the foundation for a successful career in any industry.

5. Maintaining networks and using them in the long term

5.1. Maintaining networks - the path to stable relationships

B uilding your own network is an important first step, but the true potential of a network only unfolds through targeted maintenance. Stable relationships need attention and regular contact in order to create trust and reliability. That is why we are now looking at how you can maintain your contacts in the long term, live the principle of reciprocity and thus create a network that will provide you with continuous support on your career path.

Perhaps you are wondering why regular maintenance of your own network is crucial? There are various reasons for this. Networks are constantly evolving, and relationships that are not maintained often lose intensity or disappear altogether.

Regular interaction is therefore very important in order to keep existing connections alive and deepen them. It's not just about having contacts, but developing relationships that are based on mutual added value. Through continuous maintenance, you will be remembered and your contacts will know that they can rely on you - and vice versa.

To actively nurture your contacts, make a point of keeping in touch regularly, even if it's just a quick message or a friendly update. Sharing professional developments, exciting projects or successes can help to strengthen connections and emphasize commonalities. If you continually nurture your relationships, you will have a stable network that you can fall back on at any time. This also has the positive side effect of keeping you up to date with what's going on in the professional lives of your network partners.

You should also be familiar with the principle of reciprocity. The principle of reciprocity is a cornerstone of successful long-term networking. Networking is particularly valuable when both sides feel that they can benefit and support each other. One-sided taking often leads to a loss of interest in the exchange and the relationship loses substance. By proactively contributing your own resources, knowledge and contacts, you create a basis for a balanced and stable network. Therefore: give first and try to give more than you receive. But how can you do that?

To consciously live the principle of reciprocity, you can actively look for opportunities to help others. This can be done by sharing valuable information, helping with projects or making recommendations. If you are known in your network as someone who likes to give, this strengthens your position and increases the likelihood that others will also be willing to help you when you need it. Personally, I therefore always like to follow the motto "Sharing is Caring".

Regular communication is the key to maintaining your relationships in the network. The points of contact do not necessarily have to be extensive or time-consuming - even small, personal messages can be enough to maintain the connection. A friendly greeting, a brief reference to interesting articles or current industry developments or congratulations on a professional success or milestone help to stay in touch.

An easy way to organize communication is to set reminders or keep a simple contact list where you record when you last had contact with a person. You can also use networking events or special days such as birthdays to check in and refresh the connection. By taking an interest in the successes and progress of your contacts and contacting them regularly, you show interest and ensure that you are remembered. It also makes your contact more personalized. Nowadays, there are of course various tools and apps that make this work easier for you. But you can also use other ideas.

A small gift, a handwritten letter or sharing an article that is specific to your contact's interests is a great way to build a stronger connection. Such gestures don't have to be costly or time-consuming; often simple, personal tokens of appreciation are enough to make a positive impact. In fact, one of the most important investments is the time you invest in this contact.

Furthermore, commitment is essential in order to establish trust and reliability in the network. If you make promises or offer support, it is important to keep them. Contacts in the network who can trust you and know that you are reliable will be more willing to offer you support. In any case, I believe that reliability is one of the essential qualities that are also part of business etiquette.

Therefore, make sure you keep deadlines and promises and stick to agreements. If you are unable to keep a promise, communicate openly and offer alternatives. You also want to be treated in the same way. A reliable appearance in the network will strengthen your reputation and create a solid basis for future cooperation. Avoid simply not getting in touch or replying at all costs. Ghosting is unfortunately not uncommon these days, but in my opinion it is extremely unprofessional.

Maintaining a network requires regular communication, the principle of reciprocity and small gestures of appreciation. Through continuous attention and reliability, you create long-term relationships that support you professionally and personally. Careful cultivation of your contacts forms the basis for a strong and stable network that you can always count on.

5.2. Leading your own network through times of crisis

The importance of a stable network is often particularly noticeable in times of professional and personal crisis. A well-maintained network can provide important support in difficult phases, be it through concrete assistance, access to resources or simply through emotional support. In this chapter, you will learn how to get your network through times of crisis and how you can both use it as support and continue to maintain it in order to strengthen trust and stability.

Crises, whether due to professional challenges, changes in the company or personal setbacks, can have a significant impact on your own well-being and career. At such times, it is helpful to have a network to fall back on to support you. A stable network can offer support by providing knowledge, resources and contacts, or simply by listening and offering moral support to help you get through difficult times.

In order to find support, it is advisable to openly approach trustworthy people from your network. Explain your situation and ask specifically for advice or help if you need it. People are often willing to help if they know they are really needed and a stable relationship already exists by then. Communicating your needs clearly and directly can help to avoid misunderstandings and get targeted support.

Therefore, also try to change your perspective on such difficult situations. Crises can be an opportunity to strengthen relationships and increase mutual appreciation. People who support you in difficult phases often show a high level of commitment and loyalty, which strengthens the relationship in the long term. If you notice that someone in your network is in a difficult situation, this is an opportunity to offer support yourself and deepen the connection. Often this person will then go out of their way to give you something in return. But remember that this should not be the main reason for your support.

Show solidarity. Even if you may not always be able to provide concrete help, even small gestures such as an encouraging phone call or a supportive message can have a big impact. Such mutual commitment creates a strong bond that forms a stable basis for the relationship in the long term. It may even be enough to show understanding for the other person's situation.

Share resources and contacts

In times of crisis, access to certain resources or networking with others is often crucial. If you have a well-cultivated network, you may have access to valuable contacts and information that can help you manage your situation. A well-connected colleague, an experienced mentor or a professional contact from a related industry can provide valuable perspectives and advice that can help navigate a crisis.

Don't hesitate to draw on these resources and, where appropriate, link contacts from your network if you feel it could benefit both parties. Using your contacts in this way may result in others being just as willing to share their resources with you.

Another important factor is open and honest communication. So stick to this type of communication even in times of crisis to avoid misunderstandings and maintain a basis of trust. If you find yourself in a difficult phase, it can therefore be helpful to communicate your situation and any restrictions clearly. For example, if you temporarily have less time for networking or joint projects, it is fair and professional to address this if necessary and possibly suggest alternatives.

Dealing openly with times of crisis shows that you treat your contacts honestly and respectfully. Transparency creates trust and signals that you take the relationship seriously, even when things are difficult. Even if you are seeking support from others yourself, it is important to keep the give and take in balance and, as soon as the crisis is over, show yourself to be a reliable contact again.

Once the crisis is over, it is important to turn to the people who gave you support. Show them your gratitude. You can do this by sending a personal thank you, a message or even a small gift. Showing gratitude is a way of expressing appreciation and strengthening the bond in the long term. If you decide to give a small physical token of gratitude, please note that it should really only have a small material value. In the business world in particular, gifts can often only be accepted up to a relatively small amount.

Continue to think about how you can give back what you have received. If the opportunity arises to offer your own support to the people who have helped you, this is a wonderful way to do just that. It also shows them that you don't take their support for granted. This kind of appreciation usually pleases everyone.

To summarize, your network, if stable and professionally established, can be a valuable support in times of crisis by providing you with backing, resources and moral support. Open communication and the principle of reciprocity are key to maintaining the network even in difficult times and building and maintaining trust. Be grateful for these people in your life and show it. In this way, you will create a stable network that will not only carry you through crises, but will be strengthened and consolidated in the long term.

5.3. Collaboration and opportunities through networks

A strong network not only offers support in difficult times, but also opens up numerous opportunities for collaboration, projects and professional growth. Networks can serve as a platform to foster innovative ideas and partnerships and discover new career paths. In this chapter, you will learn how you can use your network as a career and development tool through targeted collaborations and the exploitation of opportunities.

Certainly one of the most valuable functions of a network is access to information and opportunities that are not visible to everyone. New job offers, project ideas or collaborations - such opportunities often arise through informal conversations and exchanges with people from the network. Consciously recognizing and taking advantage of such opportunities can help to advance professional development and gain new experiences. These aspects are also the real career booster that you can and should strive for through networking.

To take advantage of professional opportunities, it is helpful to keep in regular contact with your contacts and ask about new developments in their professional environment. Keeping an ear open for changes and trends in your industry can enable you to become aware of exciting opportunities at an early stage. If an opportunity arises, don't be afraid to show interest and ask what collaboration or involvement might look like.

Another aspect can be collaboration. They offer the opportunity to expand your own knowledge and skills by working together with other professionals. This makes you and your knowledge even more valuable as an employee. Particularly in a professional environment, working together with other experts can lead to innovative ideas and successes that would be difficult to achieve alone. A collaborative project can be, for example, a joint research project, an event, a working group or a publication. Sometimes it can even lead to the creation of a new company. Be open to all the possibilities that can grow out of such collaborations. But how do you come to such a collaboration?

To initiate a collaboration, you can take the following approach to reach out to a person or team in your network who have similar professional goals or interests. Planning a project together not only strengthens the relationship, but also allows you to gain valuable insights and expertise from different perspectives. Define clear roles and goals for the collaboration to ensure that both sides benefit and the project is built on a solid foundation.

Trust is also essential in this context. You can also achieve this through clear communication. When working with others, it is important to clarify expectations, roles and responsibilities from the outset in order to avoid misunderstandings. Regular communication and open feedback makes collaboration more productive and helps to address and resolve conflicts or disagreements at an early stage. If your network partner trusts you, both sides will be more willing to fully engage and make the collaboration successful. Creating a positive and supportive atmosphere helps everyone involved feel comfortable and motivated to give their best.

Even if a collaboration is completed, it is worth maintaining the relationship and staying in touch. Continue to be open to new opportunities. By staying in touch after the project and showing interest in the developments and successes of your partners, you deepen the relationship and build a trusting basis for future projects.

Collaborations and opportunities in the network therefore offer you valuable possibilities for professional growth, innovative projects and new partnerships. By recognizing and taking advantage of opportunities, creating win-win situations and fostering long-term relationships, you can use your network to drive your career. Networking events, clear communication and building trust are essential elements in creating successful collaborations and realizing the full potential of your network.

If you are interested in the targeted creation of opportunities and possibilities, take a look at the keyword "serendipity". Finally, let's look at how you can keep reflecting on your network.

5.4. Reflection and further development of your network

As you already know, a strong network is not a static structure, but is constantly evolving. In order to use your network as a long-term resource and adapt it to your own career goals, it is important to regularly reflect and, if necessary, adapt it, add contacts and open up completely new fields. This is why it is now time to review the quality of your relationships, develop your network in a targeted manner and set new goals in order to utilize the full potential of your contacts.

Network according to the motto: "Quality before quantity". A large network can be valuable, but not all contacts offer long-term added value. To ensure that your network is actually conducive to your goals, you should review it at regular intervals. A targeted analysis of your contacts can help you to identify the relationships that are particularly valuable and those that may be less relevant.

Think back to the beginning of the book, when we talked about evaluating your contacts. Now we're going to do it again in a similar way. Categorize your contacts: Which people offer you valuable insight, support or access to new opportunities? Are there any relationships that have flattened out over time? Are they still important to you? This inventory will help you focus on the quality of your contacts and ensure that your energy goes into nurturing the relationships that matter most.

We also talked about gaps in your network at the beginning. It can therefore be helpful to repeat this exercise at regular intervals. This way, your network is always up to date and matches your current situation. In this respect, networking is not a science, but rather an art. It is difficult to say which contacts could be helpful in the near or medium future. You can also rely on your gut feeling here. And if you haven't made contact with someone for a while and they turn out to be relevant later on, don't despair. Make contact and revive the relationship. But don't open the door. First find out where the other person stands at the moment and what they might gain from re-establishing contact with you.

Setting new goals and perspectives for your own network work

A network is only truly effective if it is geared towards its own goals. It is therefore important to regularly set new goals for your networking activities. These goals can be, for example, increasing your visibility in a particular industry, networking with leaders or strengthening relationships within a particular network.

Define what you want to achieve through your network over the next few months and set yourself concrete steps to achieve these goals. This will give your networking more structure and focus, which will help you to work towards your career goals in a targeted manner. Even small measures, such as regularly sharing industry content or writing your own posts on social media, can help you achieve your goals in the long term and strengthen your presence in the network.

Last but not least: a successful network requires regular reflection and targeted further development. By reviewing your contacts, closing gaps and setting new goals, your network will remain adapted to your needs and career steps. Continuous learning and long-term relationships create a stable, loyal basis that will support you at every stage of your career.

I admit, taking all the steps described in this book takes time and commitment. But I can tell you that it will be worth it. Take on a lot and, above all, discover the fun of networking. You will be surprised how many interesting and exciting people you will meet. And whether you want to enjoy a cup of coffee with it is up to you. What is certain, however, is that careers (through networking) are advanced in precisely such settings. So don't miss out on this opportunity.

I wish you every success with your networking!

Do you need help with strategic network development and maintenance? Please contact me at coach@eva-tolimir.de
If this book has helped you, please rate it on Amazon.

6

6. Sources

Baltes, G., & Schmidt, C. (2012). *Life-cycle-oriented career planning: Strategies for shaping careers in different phases of life.* Springer Gabler.

Brown, B. (2018). *Dare to lead: Brave work. Tough conversations. Whole hearts.* Random House.

Cialdini, R. B. (2006). *Influence: The psychology of persuasion.* Harper Business.

Eagly, A. H., & Carli, L. L. (2007). Through the labyrinth: The truth about how women become leaders. Harvard Business Review Press.

Ferrazzi, K., & Raz, T. (2005). *Never eat alone: And other secrets to success, one relationship at a time.* Crown Business.

Granovetter, M. S. (1995). *Getting a job: A study of contacts and careers.* University of Chicago Press.

Helgesen, S., & Goldsmith, M. (2018). *How women rise: Break the 12 habits holding you back from your next raise, promotion, or job.* Hachette Books.

Hewlett, S. A. (2013). *Forget a mentor, find a sponsor: The new way to fast-track your career.* Harvard Business Review Press.

Ibarra, H. (2015). *Act like a leader, think like a leader.* Harvard Business Review Press.

Ibarra, H., Ely, R., & Kolb, D. (2013). *Taking gender into account: Theory and design for women's leadership development programs.* Academy of Management Learning & Education.

Kay, K., & Shipman, C. (2014). *The confidence code: The science and art of self-assurance - What women should know.* Harper Business.

Liebscher, A. (2019). *Behind every person is a network: Success strategies for a new world of work.* Springer Gabler.

Lipman, J. (2018). *That's what she said: What men need to know (and women need to tell them) about working together.* William Morrow.

Lublin, J. S. (2016). *Earning it: Hard-won lessons from trailblazing women at the top of the business world.* Harper Business.

Mackay, H. (1997). *Dig your well before you're thirsty: The only networking book you'll ever need.* Currency.

McKinsey & Company, & Lean In. (since 2015). *Women in the workplace.* womenintheworkplace.com.

Myers, B. (2011). *Take the lead: Motivate, inspire, and bring out the best in yourself and everyone around you.* Simon & Schuster.

Sandberg, S. (2013). *Lean in: Women, work, and the will to lead.* Knopf.

Scalise, C., & Caprino, K. (2020). *The most powerful you: 7 bravery-boosting paths to career bliss.* HarperCollins Leadership.

Tolimir, E.-M. (2022). *Lifecycle-oriented career planning: A path for women in management positions.* Springer Gabler.